This Journal Belongs To:

_____

Building Intimacy with Daily Gems
100 Questions for Couples to Start Conversations, Build Trust &
Intimacy.

Grubb
Blackwood
PUBLISHING

Introduction

Building Intimacy with daily gems was written to encourage intimacy, by increasing the communication between couples with 100 thought-provoking questions. As a couple, you will get to know each other better as you ask the questions that will help to stimulate discussion and understanding of each other resulting in a deeper bond of love.

Discussing one another's feelings in a calm and candid manner is a great way to develop a strong healthy bond with each other. These questions will help you both communicate how you are feeling, what your expectations are in the relationship and encourage one another to empathize with each other.

Bring memories alive and rekindle intimacy, as you relive the reasons why you fell in love. Ask these questions while you are both relaxing on the couch or in bed. Make eye to eye contact with each other. XOXO

Michelle and Devon Blackwood

Do What You Did In
The Beginning Of A
Relationship And There
Won't Be An End.

Anonymous

Date: /   /

Do you think you and your partner share the same values?

_____

_____

_____

_____

_____

_____

_____

_____

_____

_____

_____

_____

_____

_____

Date: / /

How do you feel about how much time you spend together?

_____

_____

_____

_____

_____

_____

_____

_____

_____

_____

_____

_____

_____

_____

_____

Date: /   /

Would you say that your partner understands what you are feeling?

_____

_____

_____

_____

_____

_____

_____

_____

_____

_____

_____

_____

_____

_____

Date: /   /

How much alone time do you need?

_____

_____

_____

_____

_____

_____

_____

_____

_____

_____

_____

_____

_____

_____

Date: /   /

The two of you are hitting the outdoors. What would you prefer to spend the day doing?

_____

_____

_____

_____

_____

_____

_____

_____

_____

_____

_____

_____

_____

_____

Date: / /

What is the best gift your partner could give you?

_____

_____

_____

_____

_____

_____

_____

_____

_____

_____

_____

_____

_____

_____

Date: /   /

What's the main way you show your love?

_____

_____

_____

_____

_____

_____

_____

_____

_____

_____

_____

_____

_____

_____

Date: / /

What makes you feel most loved?

_____

_____

_____

_____

_____

_____

_____

_____

_____

_____

_____

_____

_____

_____

_____

Date: /   /

What is the best gift you could give to your partner?

_____

_____

_____

_____

_____

_____

_____

_____

_____

_____

_____

_____

_____

_____

Date: /   /

What makes you feel appreciated?

_____

_____

_____

_____

_____

_____

_____

_____

_____

_____

_____

_____

_____

_____

Date: / /

What is one word that describes your relationship?

_____

_____

_____

_____

_____

_____

_____

_____

_____

_____

_____

_____

_____

Date: /   /

How would you describe your partner in three words, and why?

_____

_____

_____

_____

_____

_____

_____

_____

_____

_____

_____

_____

_____

_____

Date: /   /

When and how did you know that you wanted to be with your partner officially?

_____

_____

_____

_____

_____

_____

_____

_____

_____

_____

_____

_____

_____

_____

Date: /   /

Where you nervous/anxious before your first kiss? How did it happen?

_____

_____

_____

_____

_____

_____

_____

_____

_____

_____

_____

_____

_____

_____

_____

_____

Date: /   /

What is your favorite memory so far with your partner?

_____

_____

_____

_____

_____

_____

_____

_____

_____

_____

_____

_____

_____

_____

Date: / /

When did you fall in love with your partner?

_____

_____

_____

_____

_____

_____

_____

_____

_____

_____

_____

_____

_____

_____

_____

Date: /   /

How do you want your partner to express their affections for you?

_____

_____

_____

_____

_____

_____

_____

_____

_____

_____

_____

_____

_____

_____

Date: / /

How does your partner want you to express your affections for them?

_____

_____

_____

_____

_____

_____

_____

_____

_____

_____

_____

_____

_____

_____

Date: /   /

What are the things you and your partner have in common?

_____

_____

_____

_____

_____

_____

_____

_____

_____

_____

_____

_____

_____

Date: /   /

What are the things that make you and your partner different?

_____

_____

_____

_____

_____

_____

_____

_____

_____

_____

_____

_____

_____

_____

What is your favorite tradition together? Or what would be a good tradition to create, if you don't have one already?

_____

_____

_____

_____

_____

_____

_____

_____

_____

_____

_____

_____

_____

Date: / /

What are some of the strengths in your relationship?

_____

_____

_____

_____

_____

_____

_____

_____

_____

_____

_____

_____

_____

_____

Date: / /

What do you find most attractive about each other?

_____

_____

_____

_____

_____

_____

_____

_____

_____

_____

_____

_____

_____

Date: /   /

Where in the world would you want to go with your partner and why?

_____

_____

_____

_____

_____

_____

_____

_____

_____

_____

_____

_____

_____

_____

_____

Date: /   /

How have you changed since being in this relationship?

_____

_____

_____

_____

_____

_____

_____

_____

_____

_____

_____

_____

_____

_____

Date: /   /

How has your partner changed since being in this relationship?

_____

_____

_____

_____

_____

_____

_____

_____

_____

_____

_____

_____

_____

_____

_____

Date: /   /

What would you like to do with your partner that you have never done before?

_____

_____

_____

_____

_____

_____

_____

_____

_____

_____

_____

_____

_____

_____

Date: / /

Where did you and your partner meet? Describe how it happened.

_____

_____

_____

_____

_____

_____

_____

_____

_____

_____

_____

_____

_____

_____

Date: /   /

What was your first impression of your partner?

_____

_____

_____

_____

_____

_____

_____

_____

_____

_____

_____

_____

_____

Date: /   /

What is an ideal weekend for you and your partner?

_____

_____

_____

_____

_____

_____

_____

_____

_____

_____

_____

_____

_____

_____

_____

Date: / /

Which songs that you listen to that make you think of your partner?

_____

_____

_____

_____

_____

_____

_____

_____

_____

_____

_____

_____

_____

Date: /   /

What are a few date night activities that you and your partner would want to do?

_____

_____

_____

_____

_____

_____

_____

_____

_____

_____

_____

_____

_____

_____

_____

_____

Date: /   /

What do you vividly remember about your first date together?

_____

_____

_____

_____

_____

_____

_____

_____

_____

_____

_____

_____

_____

_____

Date: /   /

What are your top three turn-ons about your partner?

_____

_____

_____

_____

_____

_____

_____

_____

_____

_____

_____

_____

_____

_____

Date: /   /

What makes your relationship meaningful?

_____

_____

_____

_____

_____

_____

_____

_____

_____

_____

_____

_____

_____

Date: /   /

What's your favorite inside jokes that you share with your partner?

_____

_____

_____

_____

_____

_____

_____

_____

_____

_____

_____

_____

_____

_____

Date: /   /

What are your favorite movies and television shows that you share together?
List them below.

_____

_____

_____

_____

_____

_____

_____

_____

_____

_____

_____

_____

_____

_____

_____

Date: /   /

What are your most proud accomplishments as a couple?

_____

_____

_____

_____

_____

_____

_____

_____

_____

_____

_____

_____

_____

_____

_____

Date: /   /

What do you admire most about your partner?

_____

_____

_____

_____

_____

_____

_____

_____

_____

_____

_____

_____

_____

_____

Date: /   /

What's your idea of a perfect date?

_____

_____

_____

_____

_____

_____

_____

_____

_____

_____

_____

_____

_____

_____

_____

_____

Date: /   /

What is something you would like to do to invest in your relationship?

_____

_____

_____

_____

_____

_____

_____

_____

_____

_____

_____

_____

_____

_____

Date: /   /

What is your best romantic memory with your partner?

_____

_____

_____

_____

_____

_____

_____

_____

_____

_____

_____

_____

_____

_____

Date: /   /

What is your dream vacation that you would enjoy with your partner?

_____

_____

_____

_____

_____

_____

_____

_____

_____

_____

_____

_____

_____

_____

_____

Date: / /

What are three of the happiest moments you shared with your partner?

_____

_____

_____

_____

_____

_____

_____

_____

_____

_____

_____

_____

_____

_____

_____

Date: /   /

What are some things you and your partner can do to stay healthy?

_____

_____

_____

_____

_____

_____

_____

_____

_____

_____

_____

_____

_____

Date: /   /

What is one thing or activity that makes you feel alive together?

_____

_____

_____

_____

_____

_____

_____

_____

_____

_____

_____

_____

_____

_____

Date: /   /

What makes you and your partner feel appreciated?

_____

_____

_____

_____

_____

_____

_____

_____

_____

_____

_____

_____

_____

_____

Date: / /

Is there something that you miss, that you and your partner used to do?

_____

_____

_____

_____

_____

_____

_____

_____

_____

_____

_____

_____

_____

_____

Date: /   /

What do you wish you could spend more time doing in your relationship?

_____

_____

_____

_____

_____

_____

_____

_____

_____

_____

_____

_____

_____

Date: /   /

What are some things you would want to be complimented on more and why?

_____

_____

_____

_____

_____

_____

_____

_____

_____

_____

_____

_____

_____

_____

_____

Date: /   /

What are some things you could compliment your partner on more?

_____

_____

_____

_____

_____

_____

_____

_____

_____

_____

_____

_____

_____

_____

Date: /   /

What adventure would you like to do in the next few months with your partner?

_____

_____

_____

_____

_____

_____

_____

_____

_____

_____

_____

_____

_____

_____

_____

Date: / /

What mutual goals would you like to see you and your partner
accomplishing in the next 5 years?

_____

_____

_____

_____

_____

_____

_____

_____

_____

_____

_____

_____

_____

Date: /   /

What is the most memorable life advice you received for your relationship?

_____

_____

_____

_____

_____

_____

_____

_____

_____

_____

_____

_____

_____

_____

_____

Date: /   /

Five years from now, how do you envision your life together?

_____

_____

_____

_____

_____

_____

_____

_____

_____

_____

_____

_____

_____

_____

Date: /   /

What do you envy from other people's relationship and why?

_____

_____

_____

_____

_____

_____

_____

_____

_____

_____

_____

_____

_____

_____

_____

_____

_____

Date: /   /

What is you and your partner sexiest features and why?

_____

_____

_____

_____

_____

_____

_____

_____

_____

_____

_____

_____

_____

_____

_____

Date: /   /

On what ways do you work well together?

_____

_____

_____

_____

_____

_____

_____

_____

_____

_____

_____

_____

_____

_____

Date: /   /

On what ways do you feel satisfied in your relationship?

_____

_____

_____

_____

_____

_____

_____

_____

_____

_____

_____

_____

_____

Date: / /

How can you and your partner support each other better?

_____

_____

_____

_____

_____

_____

_____

_____

_____

_____

_____

_____

_____

_____

Date: /   /

What values are important in your relationship?

_____

_____

_____

_____

_____

_____

_____

_____

_____

_____

_____

_____

_____

Date: / /

How can you and your partner add more value to your quality time together?

_____

_____

_____

_____

_____

_____

_____

_____

_____

_____

_____

_____

_____

_____

_____

_____

Date: / /

How do you and your partner forgive each other when you face disappointments?

_____

_____

_____

_____

_____

_____

_____

_____

_____

_____

_____

_____

_____

_____

Date: /   /

What are your hopes and dreams for your children or future children?

_____

_____

_____

_____

_____

_____

_____

_____

_____

_____

_____

_____

_____

_____

Date: /   /

What has made you and your partner laugh most about during your relationship?

_____

_____

_____

_____

_____

_____

_____

_____

_____

_____

_____

_____

_____

_____

Date: /   /

What spontaneous things have you done with your partner recently? Or list your ideas below.

_____

_____

_____

_____

_____

_____

_____

_____

_____

_____

_____

_____

_____

_____

Date: /   /

What's one thing that you couldn't have done without your partner?

_____

_____

_____

_____

_____

_____

_____

_____

_____

_____

_____

_____

_____

_____

Date: /   /

What is a topic that you and your partner could feel lost in for hours?

_____

_____

_____

_____

_____

_____

_____

_____

_____

_____

_____

_____

_____

_____

_____

_____

Date: / /

Name 5 things you are grateful for in your relationship.

_____

_____

_____

_____

_____

_____

_____

_____

_____

_____

_____

_____

_____

_____

Date: /   /

How do you and your partner meet each other's emotional needs? Or how could you meet this need?

_____

_____

_____

_____

_____

_____

_____

_____

_____

_____

_____

_____

_____

Date: /   /

What improvements could you and your partner make to improve the relationship?

_____

_____

_____

_____

_____

_____

_____

_____

_____

_____

_____

_____

_____

_____

Date: /   /

What can you and your partner do to make each other feel safer in your relationship?

_____

_____

_____

_____

_____

_____

_____

_____

_____

_____

_____

_____

_____

_____

Date: /   /

What ways can you show I love you in your relationship?

_____

_____

_____

_____

_____

_____

_____

_____

_____

_____

_____

_____

_____

Date: / /

What are your favorite places to go together?

_____

_____

_____

_____

_____

_____

_____

_____

_____

_____

_____

_____

_____

_____

_____

_____

Date: /   /

Share what you love about each other in the past, present and future?

_____

_____

_____

_____

_____

_____

_____

_____

_____

_____

_____

_____

_____

_____

Date: /   /

How positively different your life is now that you have each other?

_____

_____

_____

_____

_____

_____

_____

_____

_____

_____

_____

_____

_____

_____

Date: /   /

How do you and your partner recharge apart, so that you can enjoy time together?

_____

_____

_____

_____

_____

_____

_____

_____

_____

_____

_____

_____

_____

_____

Date: /   /

What are some things you have learned from being in this relationship?

_____

_____

_____

_____

_____

_____

_____

_____

_____

_____

_____

_____

_____

_____

Date: / /

What are your favorite comfort foods that you enjoy together?

_____

_____

_____

_____

_____

_____

_____

_____

_____

_____

_____

_____

_____

_____

Date: /   /

What are some things that you have made/built together?

_____

_____

_____

_____

_____

_____

_____

_____

_____

_____

_____

_____

_____

_____

_____

_____

Date: / /

Create a bucket list together and list them below.

_____

_____

_____

_____

_____

_____

_____

_____

_____

_____

_____

_____

_____

_____

Date: / /

When did you know that each other was the one?

_____

_____

_____

_____

_____

_____

_____

_____

_____

_____

_____

_____

_____

_____

Date: / /

How do you challenge each other to grow and to succeed?

_____

_____

_____

_____

_____

_____

_____

_____

_____

_____

_____

_____

_____

_____

Date: /   /

Have you and your partner sacrificed things in order to be together? How was it worth it?

_____

_____

_____

_____

_____

_____

_____

_____

_____

_____

_____

_____

_____

_____

Date: /   /

When have you been enormously proud of each other?

_____

_____

_____

_____

_____

_____

_____

_____

_____

_____

_____

_____

_____

_____

Date:　　/　　/

What has surprised you most about this relationship?

_____

_____

_____

_____

_____

_____

_____

_____

_____

_____

_____

_____

_____

_____

Date: /   /

Have there been times where you questioned the relationship? How did you overcome that?

_____

_____

_____

_____

_____

_____

_____

_____

_____

_____

_____

_____

_____

_____

Date: /   /

How do you still love each other when you're not at your best?

_____

_____

_____

_____

_____

_____

_____

_____

_____

_____

_____

_____

_____

_____

_____

Date: /   /

What is something you have influenced each other to do?

_____

_____

_____

_____

_____

_____

_____

_____

_____

_____

_____

_____

_____

_____

Date: / /

What qualities are you drawn to in each other?

_____

_____

_____

_____

_____

_____

_____

_____

_____

_____

_____

_____

_____

_____

Date: /   /

What is one thing you will always remember about each other?

_____

_____

_____

_____

_____

_____

_____

_____

_____

_____

_____

_____

_____

Date: / /

What is one thing your partner do that gives you butterflies?

_____

_____

_____

_____

_____

_____

_____

_____

_____

_____

_____

_____

_____

_____

_____

_____

_____

Date: /   /

What is your favorite pet name for each other and why?

_____

_____

_____

_____

_____

_____

_____

_____

_____

_____

_____

_____

_____

_____

Date: /   /

What are some reasons why you love each other?

_____

_____

_____

_____

_____

_____

_____

_____

_____

_____

_____

_____

_____

_____

_____

Date: /   /

What is your and your partner's guilty pleasure?

_____

_____

_____

_____

_____

_____

_____

_____

_____

_____

_____

_____

_____

_____

Date: /   /

What is the most embarrassing naughty experience you have shared with your partner?

_____

_____

_____

_____

_____

_____

_____

_____

_____

_____

_____

_____

_____

_____

Date:　　/　　/

How has the relationship helped you to discover yourself more?

_____

_____

_____

_____

_____

_____

_____

_____

_____

_____

_____

_____

_____

Date: /   /

Describe a past good deed from your partner that meant a lot.

_____

_____

_____

_____

_____

_____

_____

_____

_____

_____

_____

_____

_____

_____

Date: / /

Name a time your partner was there for you when you really needed it.

_____

_____

_____

_____

_____

_____

_____

_____

_____

_____

_____

_____

_____

_____

_____

Date: /   /

Write some inspirational quotes that reminds you of your spouse.

_____

_____

_____

_____

_____

_____

_____

_____

_____

_____

_____

_____

_____

_____

_____